Silisia Dances

Toward Her Dream

Victoria M. Jurgens

Dedicated to Jasmine.

The beautiful ballerina who inspired
and motivated me to write this book.
You amaze me in every way.

Silisia loved to dance. When she danced, she was in her own world. She imagined the tips of her toes touching the tops of the flowers like a butterfly flying around in the garden.

Silisia often commanded her younger brother, Sanjay, to help her create and dance in the shows that she held for her Dad and Grandma. Then she recreated those shows for her aunts, uncles, and cousins at every family event. Silisia enjoyed the clapping from everyone almost as much as she liked dancing.

Silisia's dream was to dance as a Second Soloist with The National Ballet of Canada just as her mom had. Then she could dance on the big stage in Toronto, and in other cool places all around the world.

But Silisia forgot all that when Ms. Allard, the dance teacher, told her what to do. Silisia did not listen.

VICTORIA M. JURGENS

Ms. Allard said, "Excellent plié Silisia. Now class, we'll work on tendu and rond de jambe. Silisia, I said tendu not dégagé. And remember ballet hands. We are ballerinas. Okay. Tendu everyone. Make strong, straight legs. Silisia, point your toes."

Cristela, one of the other dance students, with a high-pitched voice, started to snicker. She whispered, "Silly See Ah! You're dumb. You can't get it right."

Silisia's face turned red, and her insides hurt. She hated when Ms. Allard did not hear Cristela.

Ms. Allard said, "Okay, Silisia. Arms in second position, please. No spaghetti arms allowed."

Silisia just couldn't get it right. Then she heard another snicker. Silisia's dance friend, Erin, who had red hair and freckles, was at the end of the line of fifteen dancers. She didn't hear the snickers and sneers either.

Cristela sneered, "Silly See Ah is dumb. You're a terrible dancer."

Turning around, Silisia put her fists on her hips and said, "Stop saying that!"

"Silisia, stop talking," said Ms. Allard. "Pay attention. I said second position. Feet and arms should be in second position. Remember, no spaghetti arms. Silisia. Please. Ballet hands. We are ballerinas."

Silisia's dad picked her up after class and drove to the donut shop.

"Hey, Punkin. How was the dance lesson?" Dad asked.

"Fine," said Silisia. "I don't want to talk about it."

"What happened, Punkin?"

"I want to stop dance lessons."

"But Silisia, your dream is to dance on the big stage, here in Toronto, just as your mom did," said her Dad.

"I'll never be as good as Mommy. I want to quit."

"Did you know that after we moved to Toronto, your mom would practice for hours every day so she could be a Second Soloist with The National Ballet of Canada after Sanjay was born? Keep practicing and you will achieve your dream, too," said her Dad. "What happened?"

"No, I don't remember her practicing," said Silisia. "She just danced so beautifully all the time. I was practicing dégagé. But Ms. Allard said we had to practice tendu, instead. I don't want to keep practicing tendu over and over. Again, and again! I know how to do a tendu, but Ms. Allard keeps saying *strong, straight legs and point your toes*. I wish cancer didn't make Mommy die." Tears welled up but Silisia held them in.

"I do too, Punkin. Let's have a hug and remember Mommy," said Dad as he pulled Silisia into a big bear hug. "Before you were born, Mommy was a soloist with The Winnipeg Ballet. She was so beautiful and she practiced and practiced. Every day. Practice is what it takes to dance toward your dream," whispered Dad as he kissed the top of Silisia's head.

"I don't want to talk about it," Silisia said as she walked over to the counter. She bent down and looked at the donuts behind the glass. Can I get a donut with sprinkles?"

"Of course," said Dad.

Grandma Catherine was visiting. Silisia's middle name was Catherine, and she loved sharing it with her grandmother. Grandma had taught Silisia to cook pasta, but she still wouldn't let her fry eggs and Silisia complained every time.

Grandma said, "Remember, when you are ten, you can learn to fry eggs."

"But I'm *almost* ten," said Silisia, her voice rising. "I will be ten next month. Are you coming for my birthday?"

"Of course, honey. How are dance lessons going?" asked Grandma. "I hear you have a test coming up. You must be good. That school only asks the most skilled students to take tests."

Grandma always used big words. When Silisia was seven, she didn't know what skilled meant. Dad was the smartest person Silisia knew, so she asked him.

But Silisia didn't think she was skilled. She kept getting the steps mixed up. And Cristela kept snickering. She used a high-pitched sneer to say *Silly See Ah can't dance.* Lately, Cristella would also make faces at Silisia whenever the teacher was not looking.

Silisia said, "I'm not skilled. I'm a terrible dancer! I don't want to take the stupid test."

7

Grandma was looking at Silisia strangely. It looked like she was seeing something else. Then she asked, "Can I share a story with you of when I was a little girl?"

"Oh, I love your stories! Yes, please," said Silisia. Hopefully, the story would take her mind off of that stupid test.

Grandma said, "When I was a little girl, many years ago, I was in a spelling bee competition. I was good at spelling. I read lots of books with big words in them. The teachers picked out the very best spellers in the whole school and then marched us down to the auditorium, and lined us up. There were four other schools there, too. One at a time, each contestant was asked to spell a word. If someone spelled the word wrong, then the next student had a chance to spell it correctly. The one that spelled the word wrong had to leave the competition."

"I did not practice. I thought I was the best. I thought that none of the other students could beat me at spelling. I spelled 'aardvark' right, then 'beehive', and even 'Mississippi'. But I spelled the word 'voracious' wrong. I was the first one out of the competition. I was so embarrassed. Now everyone would know how dumb I was. Wilburt, an eleven-year-old from the school in the next town, was the winner. At the end of the competition, he swaggered past me holding out his trophy."

"When I cried in my mother's arms, she told me that she loved me no matter what."

"But my older sister said, "*You should practice for the next big competition. I'll pretend to be the one asking the words. I'll dig up the biggest words I can find, and we'll practice every day.*"

"*I can't do it. I was the first one to blow it in the competition. That proves I'm dumb at spelling,*" I wailed as I grabbed a tissue and blew my nose."

"*No. You. Are. Not!*" said my sister. My sister was already fifteen, so I normally knew she had to be right. But this time, I knew she was wrong. My sister refused to believe me. She insisted that we practice every single day. There were so many days I got every word wrong. I wanted to give up."

"But my sister wouldn't let me. Sometimes when I got all the words wrong, she would bring me an oatmeal raisin cookie and a glass of milk. My sister was thoughtful that way. I love oatmeal raisin cookies. Do you like oatmeal raisin cookies, Silisia?"

"Ew, no way! I like donuts with sprinkles," said Silisia.

"Do you want to know what happened next?" asked Grandma.

Silisia was very polite and said, "Yes, of course."

"Well, in the next competition, everyone in the whole province competed. I was nearly ten years old, just like you. There were lots of schools taking part in the spelling competition, and many of the kids were older than me. Some competitors were twelve."

Silisia asked, "Were your sister and your mom there to watch you?"

"Oh yes," Grandma said. Her eyes squinted a bit, and it looked like Grandma was trying to see something far away. "They sat right up front where I could see them. My sister kept her fingers crossed. She would hold them up whenever I looked her way."

Grandma had stopped talking. Again, she was smiling, looking far away.

"Grandma, what happened?" Silisia asked.

Grandma smiled and her face lit up like the sun. The same smile her grandma had every time she saw Silisia.

"Finally, there were only two of us on stage. Wilburt, the boy that won the last competition, and me. He was grinning that same wicked grin he had on when he beat everyone in the last spelling bee."

"My insides were pinched, my throat was as dry as the desert, and my heart was beating so loud it sounded like a freight train. I looked at my sister. She held up her crossed fingers. My mom pretended to hug me. I focused on them and did not look at Wilburt."

"Then I heard him spelling the word wrong. It was wrong. I knew it was wrong!"

"I took a big breath and focused on the word. This was my chance to spell *specificity* right. I spelled it, and the whole stadium jumped to their feet and clapped when the teacher said *Catherine, you are correct. You win!*"

"My mother and sister were waving their arms and cheering. Silisia, I want you to feel that happiness too. It takes a lot of hard work to improve your skills. I know how skilled you are. I can see your potential." Grandma said.

My grandma says that a lot. Potential. Thought Silisia.

"Dream your biggest dream every day! Dream of being part of The National Ballet of Canada and dancing on the big stage in Toronto and all around the world," said Grandma, with her big sunbeam smile. "Keep practicing, Silisia. That's what it takes to dance toward your dream."

At the next dance class, Silisia listened to the teacher and stopped looking at or listening to Cristela. Silisia memorized all of the ballet positions so she could practice with Erin at home in front of the giant mirror that her dad had installed in the basement. Then they would practice at Erin's house with the barre her parents had installed for the girls to do their ballet practice.

Ms. Allard said, "I'm impressed with your ballet hands and your tendu has improved. Your fifth position is excellent. You must be practicing a lot. That is the way to become a ballerina. Practice. Practice. Practice."

Then the big test day arrived. There were butterflies in her stomach.

"Good!" said Dad, when Silisia told him about the butterflies. "They'll keep you light on your feet." Her dad gave her a big bear hug and said, "I love you no matter what. Do your best."

Sanjay said, "You can do it!", as he gave her a high five.

Silisia focused on thinking about all of the dance steps she knew, along with one happy thought. Tomorrow, she would be ten and she would fry eggs with her grandma.

Silisia smiled and whispered to herself, "You can do it."

Silisia practiced in her head and focused on how to position her hands, arms, and feet for each position as she walked steadily into the hall where two other girls were already waiting. They were also going to take the ballet exam. Silisia's stomach popped right up into her mouth when she saw Cristela.

Erin came over and hugged Silisia. "You're first. We practiced a lot. You can do it."

Then she heard Ms. Allard call out, "Now, ballerinas, come backstage and line up. No talking to each other. When the exam is over, you tell the ballerina that completed her exam *well done*. We are ballerinas and we must practice our professionalism. Go ahead, Silisia. You're first. Come back here when you're finished."

The next day, Silisia walked around wearing an ear-to-ear grin. She had passed her dance test and so did Erin. They had giggled together about how Cristella nearly choked saying *well done*.

Silisia's dad gave her lots of bear hugs. Every time she passed Sanjay, he'd jump up in the air and give her a high five.

17

Her grandma was full of sunbeam smiles.

And now she was frying eggs for breakfast.

Silisia's heart felt ready to burst. Her insides were warm and as fuzzy as the stuffy she squeezed when she needed a hug.

*I **am** dancing toward my dream,* thought Silisia. *And I'm getting there fast.*

THE END